SPQR

Books in the Life Long Ago Series

The Life Long Ago books are close-up views of ancient civilizations. Everyday life is brilliantly re-created in panoramic, authentic drawings and concise text. Each book is a rare visual experience. Each takes the reader into the reality and excitement of history and provides an extraordinary understanding of a people and their ways.

THE ROMANS in the Days of the Empire
Pictures and Text by SHANE MILLER

The mighty Roman Empire is vividly alive in the strength of these pictures. You take your seat among 45,000 spectators at the Colosseum. You follow a freedman home to his four-story apartment house and you feel the might of the Roman army as they prepare for battle.

THE CAVE DWELLERS in the Old Stone Age
Pictures and Text by RICHARD M. POWERS

The pictures burst with life and strength. You feel the tense anticipation of the hunters as they gather before the magician in the ritual cave. You know the fear as they face a live mammoth, and realize they must kill or be killed.

THE EGYPTIANS in the Middle Kingdom
Pictures by SHANE MILLER
Text by EDWARD OCHSENSCHLAGER

A fascinating trip through this ancient land where you will visit the lonely Pharaoh of Egypt, walk through the shop-lined streets of Memphis and journey past the great pyramids of Giza.

THE ATHENIANS in the Classical Period
Pictures and Text by LEONARD WEISGARD

The beauty and reality of Athens is before you in the streets of the city as you visit an instrument maker's shop, join the crowds at the Panathenaic Stadium and stand before the Parthenon.

LIFE LONG AGO

Editorial and Historical Consultant
Edward Ochsenschlager
ARCHAEOLOGIST AND LECTURER IN CLASSICS

THE ROMANS
In the Days of the Empire

SHANE MILLER

Education Consultant
Rosemary Daly
LIBRARIAN, ETHICAL CULTURE SCHOOL, NEW YORK

COWARD-McCANN
New York

0110 UP

This is a coin made almost 1,900 years ago by order of the Roman Emperor Hadrian. One side of it is decorated with a bust of Hadrian and an inscription. The inscription reads: *Emperor Caesar — Trajan — Hadrian — Augustus — High Priest of the State Religion — Supreme Civil Head of the State*. Because the inscription also tells that Hadrian was "one of the two chief magistrates of the state for the third time," we know that the coin was made in 119 A.D. The other side shows the emperor taking the hand of a kneeling woman. The inscription reads: *Restorer of the World*. The large S.C. means that the Senate voted to have the coin made.

Roman imperial coins were often small works of art. Highly skilled artists designed the dies from which they were struck. Coins were also an important means of communication. They were used to circulate official propaganda throughout the vast Roman Empire. A coin could show a scene or legend to celebrate the emperor's victories, statecraft, or generosity. An emperor could use coins to prepare public opinion for a controversial project or strengthen the morale of the people by reminding them of the ancient ideals which had made Rome great.

Wealthy and moderately wealthy Romans lived in spacious homes. They gave frequent dinner parties and took great pleasure in fine, skillfully prepared food.

At the door of a wealthy Roman's home, guests are ushered into the entrance hall by the doorkeeper. The majordomo reports their arrival to the master of the house. All is ready in the dining room. The table is in place and around it are the couches on which the host, hostess and guests will recline for dinner. The cook hands a slave boy several coins, including the coin of Hadrian, and sends him to the market for last-minute purchases. Upstairs, attendants are completing the hair arrangement of the mistress and her daughter.

3

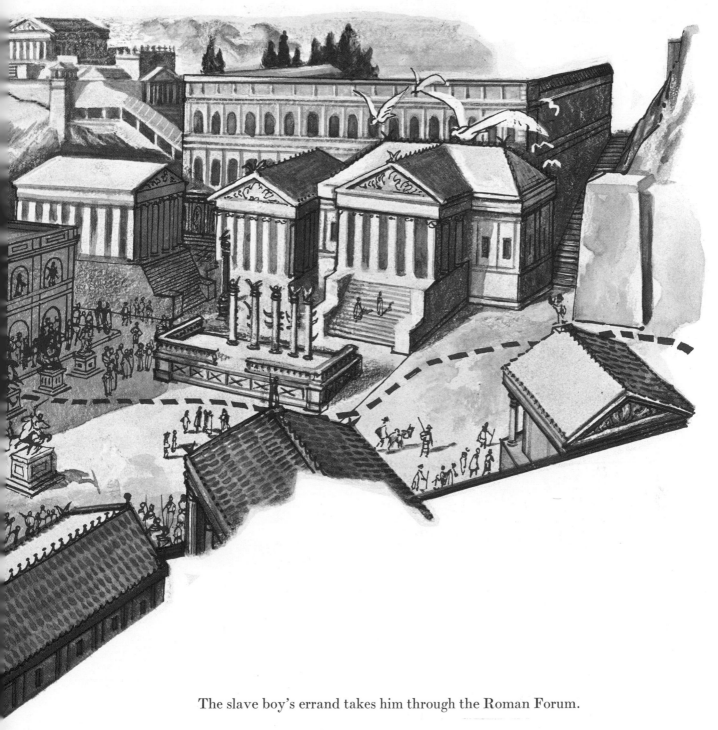

The slave boy's errand takes him through the Roman Forum.

Here at the heart of the city stood the gleaming monuments that symbolized the power and glory of Rome. These buildings, paneled in varicolored marbles and richly decorated with sculpture, formed the hub of Rome's life. In the buildings surrounding or near it, every political, religious or financial activity of the city had its place. The Forum teemed with people. Some gathered for religious ceremonies; some to watch trials at the lawcourts. Others, with nothing better to do, walked about exchanging gossip with friends and acquaintances. On days when the emperor made public speeches, distributed money, or invested foreign kings, the open spaces were so crowded that there was scarcely room to move.

The slave makes his way through the Forum of Trajan and into one of the semicircular plazas which open to either side of it. Each is bounded by a curved building with many-storied corridors and shops. Just inside, the slave trips over one of the many homeless dogs which infest the city. He falls and drops the coin. A street lounger promptly slaps his foot on it.

Rome had long ago outgrown the Roman Forum. More space was needed for official business, civic functions, marketing and free ground which the citizens might enjoy. The Forum of Trajan was the largest and most magnificent addition. A masterpiece of architecture and engineering, it was the most costly monument of ancient Rome. Twenty-four million cubic feet of earth and rock were moved to make room for it. When completed, the Forum opened a badly needed new line of communication between two halves of a city with a population of nearly two million.

The street lounger heads for the nearest wineshop with the coin.

The wineshops of Rome had counter tops fitted with holes into which large terra-cotta jars filled with wine were fitted for easy handling. The shops had tables and seats where thirsty Romans could sit and drink wine with their friends. Here also they could buy wine in large quantities for home use. The Romans classified wine by its color. They recognized four kinds: white, brown, light red and dark red. Some of their most expensive vintages took twenty years to reach maturity.

The wine seller is one of the thousands who go to the gladiatorial games at the Flavian Amphitheatre the next day.

Men and women from all walks of life attended the circus games in the Flavian Amphitheatre or Colosseum as it was later known. The games helped to keep the leisured class amused and out of mischief. The most popular were wild animal fights and gladiatorial combats. In these combats criminals and slaves fought against each other or against wild beasts.

The emperors also provided free chariot races, prizefights and athletic games for the populace.

Since the gladiator whom the wine seller favored has lost, he pays off his bet with his neighbor.

The Colosseum was a masterpiece of architectural ingenuity. Three tiers of seats and standing room above provided room for 45,000 spectators. The entrances, passages and staircases were so skillfully arranged that each person could reach his seat without trouble or confusion. A huge awning, worked by sailors, was provided for the people's comfort. It was raised, during the course of the day, over those parts of the Colosseum in the direct path of the sun.

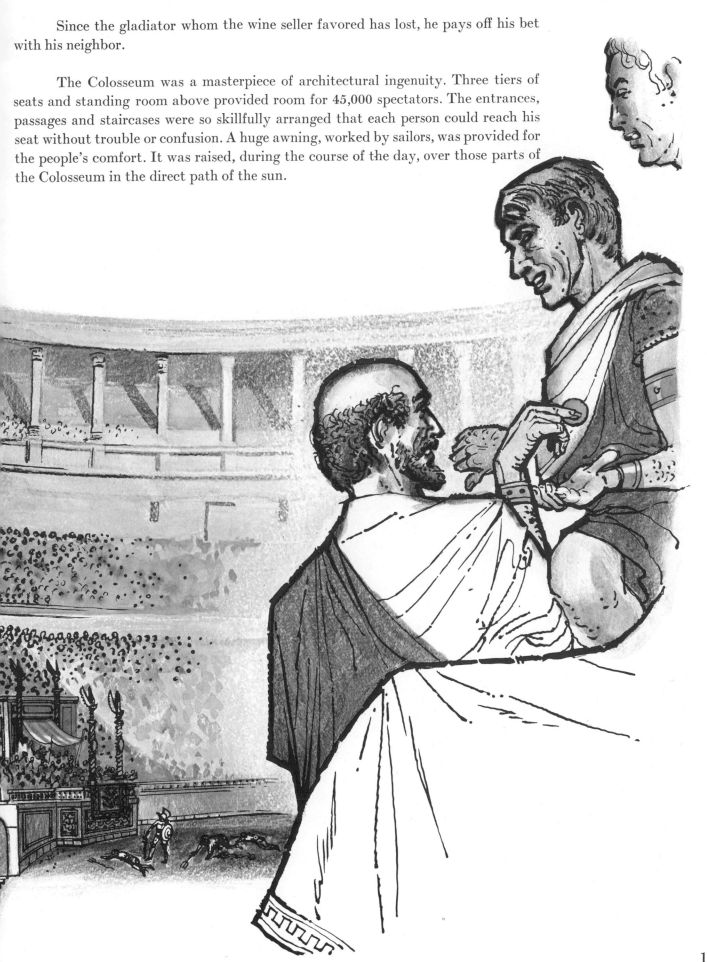

After his bath the following day, the bet winner drops the coin into the hand of the freedman who rubbed him down. The *stragili* (scrapers) used for removing sweat or oil hang over the freedman's arm.

The original purpose of the baths was cleanliness and bodily health, but they were also places of amusement. After greeting his friends and exchanging gossip, the bather read the *acta diurna,* or daily news. Next he prepared for his bath by walking in the beautifully landscaped grounds or participating in sports or gymnastics. Then began the elaborate bathing routine: first, a perspiration or hot-air bath with a gentle oil massage; second, a hot-water bath; third, a drying out in a warm room; fourth, a cold plunge; and finally the rubbing down with oil.

The many slaves and servants who worked in the baths could appear wherever needed, by means of passages underground, without crossing the halls and without bothering the bathers.

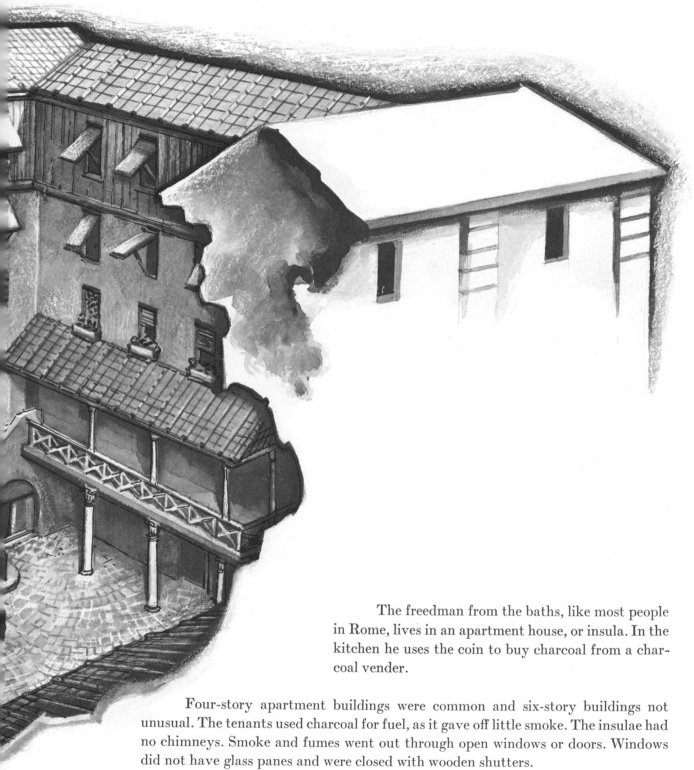

The freedman from the baths, like most people in Rome, lives in an apartment house, or insula. In the kitchen he uses the coin to buy charcoal from a charcoal vender.

Four-story apartment buildings were common and six-story buildings not unusual. The tenants used charcoal for fuel, as it gave off little smoke. The insulae had no chimneys. Smoke and fumes went out through open windows or doors. Windows did not have glass panes and were closed with wooden shutters.

Water was usually carried from a public fountain (supplied by an aqueduct). Some insulae had a direct water supply, but only for the first story, which was rented to a man of great wealth and position.

The houses had no plumbing in the upper stories. The residents depended on chamber pots, cess trenches in neighboring alleys or, for a small fee, the large and opulent public toilets. Many of these were marble paneled, decorated with statues and provided with playing fountains. They were, however, public in every sense.

The charcoal seller stops at a cookshop to buy a meat pastry. He eats quickly, for darkness is fast approaching. Hurrying away, he leaves the coin in payment on the counter in full view of a destitute sailor loitering nearby.

The city did not have street lamps. Unless the moon shone it was plunged into darkness when the sun went down. The streets twisted and turned. They were narrow — sometimes barely wide enough for three men to walk abreast. At night the Roman preferred to stay at home.

When the charcoal vender leaves, the sailor pounces on the coin. The shop owner and his wife summon the *vigili*, or policemen, who capture the sailor. At the *excubitorium,* the neighborhood police station, the sailor is brought to trial and the coin offered in evidence.

In ancient Rome, the vigili were both policemen and firemen. They made their rounds equipped with water buckets and axes for fighting fires, but were also responsible for capturing lawbreakers. The emperor had divided the vigili into seven groups, or cohorts, each under the command of a tribune. Every cohort had its own barracks, or stations, and was responsible for two districts of the city. At the head of the police force was the prefect of the night patrol. He was responsible for trying the criminals captured. Often, because of the large number of cases, the prefect delegated a part of his judicial authority to a deputy.

Next morning the deputy leaves Rome with the coin in his pocket. He is traveling to Gaul (modern France) where he owns property.

The Via Flaminia, like all roads leading out of Rome, was lined with tombs. Well-to-do Romans buried their dead in elaborate family or individual mausolea. Persons of moderate means formed clubs and erected columbaria, huge communal tombs, for their members. The poor were buried in pits in a public cemetery.

The state made, owned and maintained the main roads of the Roman Empire. The emperor appointed commissioners to superintend them and look after necessary repairs. Stone pillars were set up at each Roman mile to mark distances. Roads made rapid communication between all parts of the empire possible, facilitated the movement of armies and supplies, and promoted trade.

A cloudburst forces the deputy and his driver off the highway, just outside Lugdunum, or Lyon in modern France. They turn in at the nearest *caupona* (small hostel) for the night. The tribune flings his coin to the landlord in payment.

Roman travelers of rank avoided staying at these cauponae, for they and their landlords had an evil reputation. The accommodations were simple, a bare room for the traveler on the second floor, and a stall for his animals below.

Usually a Roman of position would plan his trip in stages, so that he could stay with friends along his route. When this was impossible, he would often camp along the road with a tent and furniture he carried with him.

There were hotels in the towns, and good hotels could be found in the large cities. The general standard was low, however, because most well-to-do Romans avoided them.

Several days later a trader stops at the caupona. When he leaves, the landlord follows him to look at his rich store of luxuries and novelties. After much bargaining, he buys a comb for his daughter. Once again the coin changes hands.

At Colonia Agrippina (modern Cologne), the merchant gives the coin to a centurion and is quickly cleared for his journey across the Rhine River. Once he has passed out of the fortress he will be on his own, for Roman protection ends here.

The "Roman Peace" was guaranteed by the well-drilled Roman army which guarded the frontiers. The generals had their recruits drilled twice daily and the whole army was trained in swimming, running, leaping, javelin throwing and sword-play. The soldiers marched twenty miles, three times a month, in full battle dress. Discipline was strict and punishment severe.

The army had other duties as well. The soldiers were often used for police and patrol. Frequently they built and maintained roads, bridges and public buildings. A soldier was seldom idle.

The centurion and his men are being trans-
ferred to Hadrian's Wall in Britain. The soldiers march
to the coast, and now ships carry them through the
choppy waters of the Channel.

The Roman navy was not maintained primarily to fight enemy fleets. By the mere fact of its existence it discouraged other nations from attempting to form a rival naval force. Its main duties were to protect the trade routes, carry important people and dispatches from place to place, and transport army units. The sailors could also be used for duties ashore. Sailors, for instance, had just finished their part in the construction of a system of fortifications in Britain.

The centurion and soldiers arrive at their station.

The wall of Hadrian was over 75 miles long, reaching from the Solway to the mouth of the Tyne River. It was twenty feet high and six to eight feet broad. Behind the wall, and separated from it by a road, was another wall of earth. Fourteen large camps were situated at intervals along the fortifications and each "mile-tower" had a contingent of soldiers on constant duty. Outside the camps, settlements sprang up where camp followers gathered.

For the most part, Roman soldiers were stationed in the same quarters for long periods of time. The soldier was expected to serve for twenty-five years, and during that time regular marriage was denied him. In practice, however, he generally married a native woman who lived in the neighboring settlement. When he was released from the army his marriage was legally recognized. The soldier would then settle in the community where he had passed so much of his life, and his children would enlist in the army as a matter of course. Army service thus became an hereditary profession.

These camp settlements helped spread Roman culture throughout the empire. Each was a little Rome with its baths, forum and theatre. They grew to great size and were the origin of many modern cities.

The night the new troops arrive, the Picts attack the wall. Awakened by the alarm sounded by the company trumpeter, the centurion leaps to his feet but before he can grab his sword he is knocked senseless by one of the barbarians. The Pict quickly searches the centurion for anything of value. He removes the coin from the centurion's belt.

Next day the prisoners are lined up, counted, and chained hand and foot. Prisoners of war are a traditional source of slaves. They are turned over to a labor procurer, or slave dealer, who has a contract for supplying men to work in the tin mines in Cornwall. All through the long march south to Cornwall, the Pictish slave keeps the coin hidden in his mouth. Eventually he is assigned to an ore raft.

The only hope of escape for slaves working the tin mines was to be assigned as crew to the huge rafts used to float ore to southern Gaul, or France. This was risky business; storms were sudden and frequent, but the Roman concern was for the valuable cargo.

29

The Pict was assigned to a raft but this was one of the unlucky voyages. A few pieces of wreckage were washed up on the Spanish coast. Among them was the coin. It found its way into the hands of an innkeeper, who gave it as change to an inspector general. The general, making rounds of inspection in Spain by coach, is now crossing the Alcántara Bridge over the Tagus River.

The bridge was built by the Army in Trajan's time. It was 670 feet long and rose 210 feet above the stream. It crossed the river on six arches. Each of the two central arches had a span of about 87 feet. The Romans were justly famous for their engineering ability. The bridge was repaired in 1860 and is still in use today.

The inspector general and his aides, now mounted on horseback, ride into the camp of the VII Gemina Legion.

When possible, the Romans built their fortified camps on slopes so they faced downhill. It was important that wood, water and food be within easy reach. The headquarters and four corners of the camp were first marked with flags. Then the soldiers set to work. They were thoroughly experienced in fortifying a camp and each man knew his exact job.

A ditch was dug around an oblong enclosure about 2,100 feet wide and 2,800 feet long. Inside the ditch the soldiers built a rampart of earth and on top of this a stockade of wooden stakes. Every soldier from general to recruit had his proper living quarters within the camp. Indeed, the camp was an improvised city with a market place, artisan quarter and judgment seat.

All Roman camps were laid out according to the same general plan.

1. Main Road
2. Left Gate
3. Right Gate
4. Imperial Gate
5. Tithe Gate
6. Quintana Road
7. Sacularis Road
8. Wall Road
9. Commander's Quarters
10. Imperial Road
11. Reviewing Stand
12. Altars
13. Commander's Personal Staff
14. Staff Officers
15. Commander's Lifeguards and Aids
16. Regular Cavalry
17. Regular Infantry
18. Officer's Quarters
19. Hospital for Men
20. Hospital for Horses
21. Marines
22. Scouts
23. Prisoners, Hostages and Plunder
24. Guards
25. Infantry and Cavalry Combined
26. Provincial Infantry Battalions
27. Barbarian Troops

The inspector general calls for a courier to deliver his report to Rome. He gives the man, as a good-luck gift, the coin of Hadrian.

The emperors maintained an imperial communications network. Army messengers were chosen from among the scouts or the supply officers. A messenger with his dispatch traveled by horse and he traveled at public expense. Only a man who carried a passport bearing the emperor's seal was entitled to this service. Provincial governors and special representatives of the emperor always carried a number of such passports, but they were dated and could be used only during a limited period.

The messenger arrives in the harbor of Ostia, the port for Rome. The ship he sailed aboard was a fast one, averaging over 100 miles a day.

The harbor at Ostia was man-made. A large section of the coastline had been dug out, and a retaining wall built around the excavated area. Then the seawater was let into it. Huge moles were constructed on each side of the entrance. Between the moles an island was built and a light tower raised above it.

Products of the whole world flowed into this port in great quantities. Ships from faraway places crowded the docks, bearing frankincense and perfumes from Arabia, silk from China, grain from Egypt, spices and gems from India, amber from the Baltic, and hundreds of other cargos. Ostia had vast warehouses where all these products were stored and from which they were distributed.

An Egyptian sailor talks the messenger into a game of chance. They furtively join a group of players on the stairway of an apartment house. The messenger loses the coin.

Romans had a passion for gambling. They played a dice game in which the dice were rolled from a box — heads or tails, odd or even — as well as backgammon and a kind of chess. Games of chance were forbidden by the emperors except during a festival, the Saturnalia, at the end of December. The penalty was four times the value of the stakes. Betting was legal at all times if wagers were made at the circus, stadium or chariot races.

The next day a grain ship draws out of Ostia bound for Alexandria. Aboard is the Egyptian sailor who won the coin from the messenger.

The average grain ship could carry a load of fifty tons but some were so large that 1,200 tons of grain could be stored in their hulls. The sea was treacherous and many ships were sunk before reaching their destinations. But if a ship arrived safely, its owner could make a fortune.

The ship safely reaches the harbor of Alexandria. During the voyage the sailor has lost the coin in another game of chance. The winner is a scholar on his way to study in Alexandria's great library.

The city, named for her founder, Alexander the Great, was the crossroads of the world. The Red Sea Canal connected Alexandria with India. The location of the city was a natural bridge between Asia and Africa, and to the south stretched the Nile River and Egypt. There were two harbors at Alexandria separated by a causeway. It was the center of trade for exotic merchandise from the East. Also, most of Rome's grain supply was grown in Egypt and shipped from Alexandria.

Egypt was a part of the Roman Empire. In fact, it was a personal possession of the emperor. He was ruler of the land and owner of all it contained. The movement of people and goods into and out of the country was strictly controlled.

The scholar gives the coin to the son of the ship's captain. The boy has just brought the scholar's baggage. The ship will soon set sail again, this time to trade along the coast of Africa.

The city of Alexandria was inhabited by people from all over the world. There were Egyptians and Romans, Greeks, Jews, Ethiopians, Arabians, Bactrians, Scythians, Persians, Libyans and a few Indians. Alexandrine citizenship was much sought after in Egypt and the emperors granted it sparingly. It afforded the citizen special privileges and was the first step to Roman citizenship. Ordinary Egyptians were forbidden to marry even a freedman of an Alexandrian citizen.

The library in Alexandria was famous. It was the first institution of its kind ever built. Here was gathered the largest collection of books in the ancient world. For over four hundred years this was the most learned spot on earth.

44

The coin finds its way into the hands of a merchant. He is engaged in trade with the inland North African cities. His caravan halts before the gates of Thamugadi, where he pays for the right to water his camels, using the coin of Hadrian.

In the year 100 A.D. the Emperor Trajan ordered the city of Thamugadi, modern Timgad, to be built on the site of a fortified post in Numidia. The city was laid out on the plan of the Roman army camp. Trajan stationed a legion of Parthian veterans in the new city. Situated at the intersection of six roads, the city soon became one of the most prosperous in North Africa. The citizens erected a theatre seating 4,000 people, a huge market, magnificent temples, a library and many public baths. When the city outgrew its original rectangular shape, a great temple was built outside the walls. The surrounding country was very fertile and agriculture was the basis of the city's wealth.

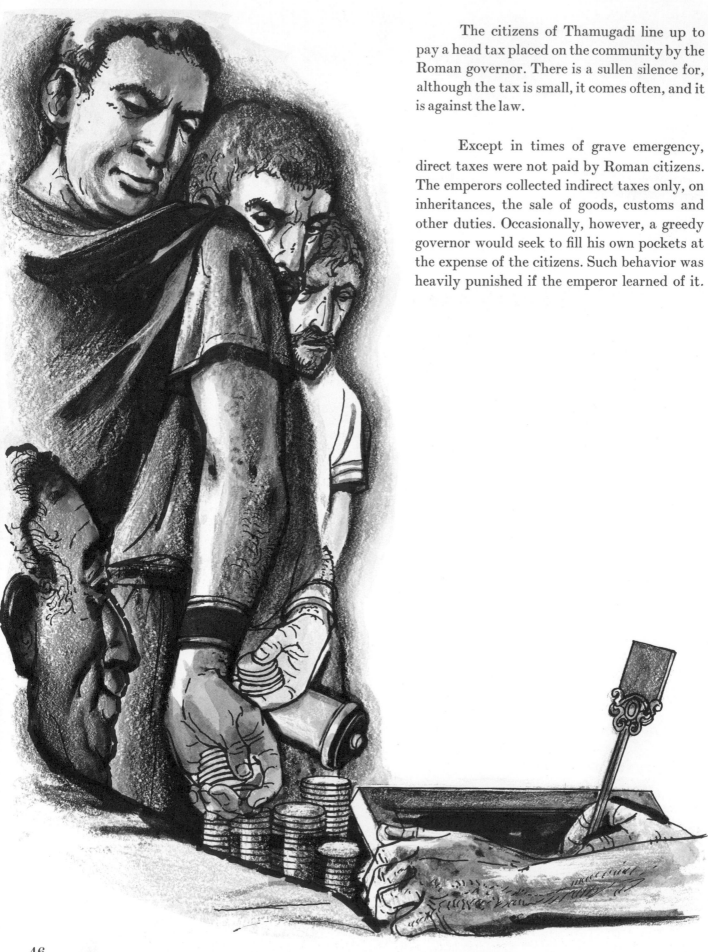

The citizens of Thamugadi line up to pay a head tax placed on the community by the Roman governor. There is a sullen silence for, although the tax is small, it comes often, and it is against the law.

Except in times of grave emergency, direct taxes were not paid by Roman citizens. The emperors collected indirect taxes only, on inheritances, the sale of goods, customs and other duties. Occasionally, however, a greedy governor would seek to fill his own pockets at the expense of the citizens. Such behavior was heavily punished if the emperor learned of it.

The Governor of Numidia is on his way to Rome. He has been recalled by Hadrian. The governor has been informed of the charges against him, but thinks he will be able to bribe his judges and the court officials with the great wealth he has amassed. He stands on the deck of the ship arrogantly flipping the coin into the air and catching it. He has no fear for his reception at Hadrian's villa.

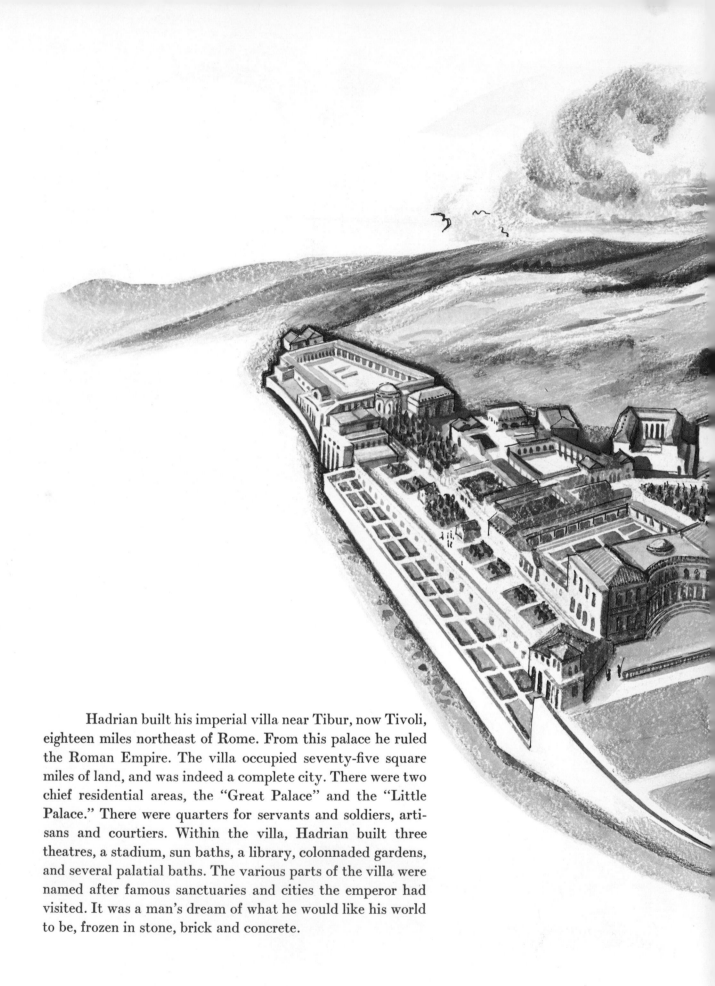

Hadrian built his imperial villa near Tibur, now Tivoli, eighteen miles northeast of Rome. From this palace he ruled the Roman Empire. The villa occupied seventy-five square miles of land, and was indeed a complete city. There were two chief residential areas, the "Great Palace" and the "Little Palace." There were quarters for servants and soldiers, artisans and courtiers. Within the villa, Hadrian built three theatres, a stadium, sun baths, a library, colonnaded gardens, and several palatial baths. The various parts of the villa were named after famous sanctuaries and cities the emperor had visited. It was a man's dream of what he would like his world to be, frozen in stone, brick and concrete.

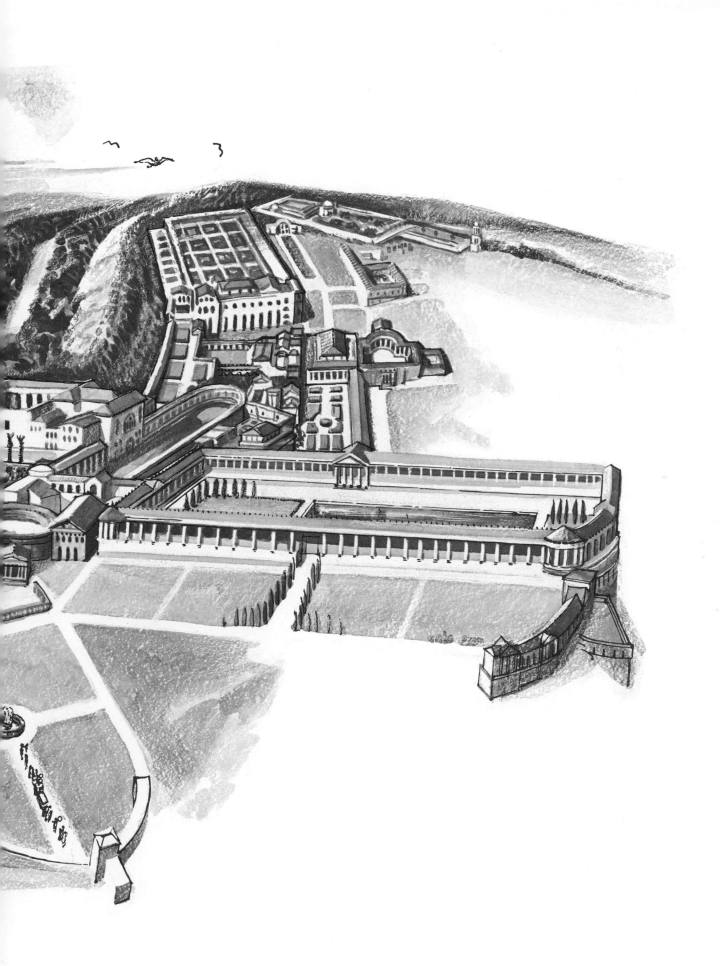

As soon as the governor arrives in Rome he makes his way to Hadrian's villa, where he greets the emperor. Hadrian turns his back, and the ex-governor is remanded to the Senate for trial.

All criminal justice was under the personal direction of the emperor, and either he or the Senate might try important cases. The Senate attempted to keep jurisdiction over its own members. Hadrian, except in military matters, usually granted them this right.

The ex-governor's trial takes place in the Curia, or Senate building, located in the Roman Forum. The presiding consul sits on the dais, with the lesser magistrates on either side of him. The sacred fire has been lighted before the statue of Victory, and the auspices have been taken. That is, an augur has officially proclaimed that the will of the gods is favorable. The evidence has already been taken by a special board of judges. The jury consists of the whole Senate. The governor's lawyers spend three days in extended oratory, hoping to influence the Senate's vote.

But in vain. The governor is sentenced to pay a huge fine, so large, indeed, that he is a ruined man. He loses property and holdings as well. Banishment to Asia Minor will follow.

Not until the trial is over and everyone has gone home is the coin found again.
The slave who cleans up the meeting hall of the Senate finds the coin under
the chair where the governor had sat. Without knowing the journey the coin has taken
all over the Roman Empire, the slave goes forth happily to spend it in the very city
from which it had started out!

ROMAN GODS

The names of their Greek counterparts are in parentheses.

JUPITER (Zeus) — the father of the gods and the god of the sky and heavenly phenomena. Usually shown holding the thunderbolt in right hand, scepter in left hand.

JUNO (Hera) — the wife of Jupiter. She was the goddess of childbirth, the protectress of the Roman matron and as the queen of the gods, the protectress of all the Roman people. Generally represented with a scepter surmounted by a cuckoo and a pomegranate.

VESTA (Hestia) — the goddess of fire in every Roman's hearth and the goddess of fire used in religious ceremonial. Seldom represented.

MARS (Ares) — primarily the god of war, but he maintained some traces of his original role as a god of agriculture. Usually shown with spear.

CERES (Demeter) — the goddesss of grain and agriculture. Generally seen crowned with a ribbon, in her hands ears of corn or a torch.

VULCAN (Hephaestus) — the god of fire and the smith of the gods. Generally shown with conical headgear, in his hands a hammer, tongs, bellows.

NEPTUNE (Poseidon) — the god of the sea and of horses. Generally shown with the trident.

VENUS (Aphrodite) — the goddess of love and beauty. Usually represented as a beautiful young girl.

MINERVA (Athena) — the goddess of defensive war and wisdom. She was the protectress of schools, commerce and industry. Usually shown with the aegis (a short goatskin cloak with zigzag edges), spear and shield.

MERCURY (Hermes) — the god of merchants. He presided over commerce. He was also messenger of the gods. Generally represented with a round winged hat, winged sandals, and a winged staff entwined with serpents.

APOLLO (Apollo) — the god of prophecy, archery, music, and the patron of young men. Usually shown with either the lyre, the bow and quiver, or the shepherd's crook.

DIANA (Artemis) — the goddess of hunting, wild animals, and the patroness of young women. Generally represented carrying a bow and quiver, and accompanied by a dog or doe.

ORCUS or DIS [dēs] (Hades) — the god of the underworld and ruler of the dead. Never represented.

PROSERPINA [prŏ·sŭr′pĭ·nă] (Persephone) — the queen of the underworld and wife of Hades. Usually represented with the bat and pomegranate.

54

AESCULAPIUS
[es′kū·lā′pǐ·ŭs]
(Asclepius)

— the god of medicine. Usually shown with the snake.

SATURN

— worshiped as a mythical king of Italy who ruled in "the golden age." He was an agricultural deity and the personification of abundance.

JANUS [jä′nŭs]

— the god and protector of doorways and gates, the god of the beginnings, and of all means of communication. Represented as a man with two faces, one looking forward, the other backward.

MANES [mā′nēz]

— the good spirits of dead ancestors.

LEMURES [lěm′ū·rēz]

— the ghosts of the dead which returned to earth to torment the living.

GENII

— the spirits which protected individual human beings from birth to death, groups of people and the places of group activities. There were unlimited numbers of these spirits in Roman religion. The most important cults were associated with the Genius of the Roman People and the Genii of the emperors.

LARES [lā′rēz]

— the spirits which protected the household and its prosperity.

PENATES [pě·nā′tēz]

— the spirits which protected the storeroom containing the food of the household.

A CHRONOLOGY OF IMPERIAL ROME

27 B.C.   Augustus became the first emperor of Rome.

29 A.D.   Jesus of Nazareth was crucified in Jerusalem.

64 A.D.   Rome was swept by fire and the Christians were accused of causing it. A vicious persecution of the Christians began.

68 A.D.   Nero, the last of the Julio-Claudian emperors, committed suicide. In the following year four emperors claimed the throne and Rome was plunged into civil war.

70 A.D.   Following a zealot revolt in Palestine, Titus destroyed Jerusalem and scattered the Jews.

117–138 A.D.   At the death of Trajan, Hadrian became emperor of Rome. Under Trajan the Roman Empire had reached its furthest extent. Hadrian gave up some of Trajan's conquests. He reorganized the army by introducing sound discipline, established a federal civil service system, extended citizenship to many provincials and encouraged learning.

161–180 A.D.   Marcus Aurelius, the philosopher emperor, fought the Parthians in the East, and barbarians on the Danube frontier. A devastating plague swept the Empire.

193 A.D.   Commodus, the last emperor of the Antonine Dynasty, was strangled to death. Civil war followed. The Romans became so depraved that Didius Julianus bought the throne at public auction.

212 A.D.   Caracalla extended Roman citizenship to all free inhabitants of the Empire.

235–285 A.D.   In fifty years of civil war, twenty-six emperors were recognized in Rome. Of these, only one, Tetricus I, escaped a violent death.

249–251 A.D.   Trajan Decius began a systematic attempt to exterminate Christianity.

253–260 A.D.   Germanic tribes invaded Gaul, the Goths invaded the area now called the Balkans and Asia Minor, and the Persians invaded Syria.

260 A.D.   The Persians captured the Emperor Valerian alive.

270–275 A.D.   Aurelian reconquered Asia Minor, Egypt and Gaul. He abandoned Dacia and built protective fortifications around Rome.

284–305 A.D.   Diocletian reorganized the Empire and appointed Maximian as co-emperor.

313 A.D.   Constantine and Licinius issued the Edict of Milan which placed Christianity on an equal footing with the state's pagan cults.

330 A.D.   Constantine moved the capital of the Empire to Constantinople (modern Istanbul).

A CHRONOLOGICAL LIST OF ROMAN EMPERORS TO CONSTANTINE

27 B.C.–14 A.D.	AUGUSTUS — Gaius Julius Caesar Octavianus	
A.D.		
14–37	TIBERIUS — Tiberius Claudius Nero Caesar	The Julio-Claudian Dynasty
37–41	CALIGULA — Gaius Julius Caesar Germanicus	
41–54	CLAUDIUS — Tiberius Claudius Drusus Nero	
54–68	NERO — Nero Claudius Caesar Drusus Germanicus	
69	GALBA — Servius Sulpicius Galba	
69	OTHO — Marcus Salvius Otho	
69	VITELLIUS — Aulus Vitellius	
69–79	VESPASIAN — Titus Flavius Sabinus Vespasianus	The Flavian Dynasty
79–81	TITUS — Titus Flavius Sabinus Vespasianus	
81–96	DOMITIAN — Titus Flavius Domitianus	
96–98	NERVA — Marcus Cocceius Nerva	
98–117	TRAJAN — Marcus Ulpius Trajanus	
117–138	HADRIAN — Publius Aelius Hadrianus	
138–161	ANTONINUS PIUS — Titus Aelius Hadrianus Antoninus	The Antonine Dynasty
161–180	MARCUS AURELIUS — Marcus Aelius Aurelius Verus	
161–169	LUCIUS VERUS — Lucius Aurelius Verus (co-emperor with Marcus Aurelius)	
180–193	COMMODUS — Lucius Aelius Aurelius Commodus	
193	PERTINAX — Publius Helvius Pertinax	
193	DIDIUS JULIANUS — Marcus Didius Salvius Julianus	
193–211	SEPTIMIUS SEVERUS — Lucius Septimius Severus	The Severan Dynasty
211–217	CARACALLA — Marcus Aurelius Antoninus	
211–212	GETA — Lucius (or Publius) Septimius Geta (co-emperor with Caracalla)	
217–218	MACRINUS — Marcus Opellius Macrinus	
218–222	ELAGABALUS or HELIOGABALUS — Marcus Aurelius Antoninus	Restoration of Severan Dynasty
222–235	SEVERUS ALEXANDER — Marcus Aurelius Severus Alexander	
235–238	MAXIMIUS I — Gaius Julius Verus Maximinus	
238	GORDIANUS AFRICANUS I — Marcus Antonius Gordianus	
	GORDIANUS AFRICANUS II — Marcus Antonianus Gordianus	
238	BALBINUS — Decimus Caelius Balbinus	
	PUPIENUS — Marcus Clodius Pupienus Maximus (co-emperors)	
238–244	GORDIANUS III (PIUS) — Marcus Antonius Gordianus	
244–249	PHILIP I — Marcus Julius Philippus	
249–251	TRAJAN DECIUS — Gaius Messius Quintus Traianus Decius	
251–254	TREBONIANUS GALLUS — Gaius Vibius Trebonianus Gallus	
253–254	AEMILIAN — Marcus Aemilius Aemilianus	
253–260	VALERIAN —Publius Licinius Valerianus	
253–268	GALLIENUS — Publius Licinius Valerianus Egnatius Gallienus	
260–261	MACRIANUS I — Marcus Fulvius Macrianus	
259–267	POSTUMUS — Marcus Cassianus Latinus Postumus	
265–270 (?)	VICTORINUS — Marcus Piavvonius Victorinus	
267–273	TETRICUS I — Gaius Pius Esuvius Tetricus I	
	TETRICUS II — Gaius Pius Esuvius Terticus II (co-emperors)	
268–270	CLAUDIUS II GOTHICUS — Marcus Aurelius Claudius	
270	QUINTILLUS — Gaius Marcus Aurelius Claudius Quintillus	
270–275	AURELIAN — Lucius Domitius Aurelianus	
275–276	TACITUS — Marcus Claudius Tacitus	
276	FLORIANUS — Marcus Annius Florianus	
276–282	PROBUS — Marcus Aurelius Carus	
282–283	CARUS — Marcus Aurelius Carus	
283–285	CARINUS — Marcus Aurelius Carinus	
283–284	NUMERIAN — Marcus Aurelius Numerianus	
284–305	DIOCLETIAN — Gaius Aurelius Valerius Diocletianus	
286–305	MAXIMIANUS I — Marcus Aurelius Valerius Maximianus	
305–306	CONSTANTIUS I — Flavius Valerius Constantius	
305–311	GALERIUS — Gaius Galerius Valerius Maximianus	
306–307	SEVERUS II — Flavius Valerius Severus	
306–312	MAXENTIUS — Marcus Aurelius Valerius Maxentius	
307–324	LICINIUS I — Publius Flavius Galerius Valerius Licianus Licinius	
306–337	CONSTANTINE I (THE GREAT) — Flavius Valerius Aurelius Constantinus	

FOR FURTHER READING

Coolidge, Olivia, *Roman People*; illus. by Lino Lipinsky. Houghton, 1959
Stories presenting various types from the aristocrat to the slave

Cowell, F. R., *Everyday Life in Ancient Rome*. Putnam, 1961
A book that covers all classes of Roman society through many periods of history

Davis, William Stearns, *A Day in Old Rome*. Allyn and Bacon, 1925
Rome at the time of Hadrian. Food, clothing, shelter, religion, costumes and customs, education, trade and government

Hadas, Moses, compiler, *A History of Rome: From Its Origins to* A.D. *529 as Told by the Roman Historians*. Doubleday Anchor, 1956

Johnston, Mary, *Roman Life*. Scott, 1957

Kirtland, G. B., *One Day in Ancient Rome*. Harcourt, 1961
A really amusing book detailing daily life in the home of a rich man

Mills, Dorothy, *The Book of the Ancient Romans*. Putnam, 1927
A general historical account of the Romans from their beginning to 476 A.D.

Robinson, Charles Alexander, *The First Book of Ancient Rome;* pictures by John Mackey. Watts, 1959
Brief, factual account of Rome from its beginnings to the fall of the Empire

Taylor, Duncan, *Ancient Rome*. Roy, 1960
A brief history beginning with Aeneas to the fall of Rome

Treble, H. A., and King, K. M., *Everyday Life in Rome;* photographs. Oxford, 1930
A good introductory book emphasizing clothing, shelter, religion, education, trade and government in the time of Caesar and Cicero

Williamson, Joanne S., *The Eagles Have Flown;* illus. by George Fulton. Knopf, 1957
An historical novel for young people set in Rome immediately following Caesar's funeral

Winterfeld, Henry, *Detectives in Togas*. Harcourt, 1956
A mystery story set in a Roman boy's school

INDEX

This is a partially annotated Index. Where no annotation occurs, the text is fully explanatory. Italics have been used for Roman words. Italic numerals designate page reference to pictures.

Africa, 41, 45

Alcantara Bridge, *30*, 31, *31*

Alexander the Great [King of Macedon, 336–323 B.C.], 41

Alexandria, 39, 40, *40*, 41, *41*, 42, *42*, 43, *43*

Alexandrine citizenship, 42

Amber [yellow fossil resin used to make beads], 37

Aqueduct [masonry channel through which water is conducted. There were 10 in Rome and many others throughout the Roman Empire at the time of Hadrian], 15

Asia, 41, 52

Augur [to foretell or indicate an issue], 52

Auspices [an omen as to the future], 52

Baths [brick and concrete buildings, either public or private], 12, *12*, 13, *13*, 27, 45, 48

Books [papyrus scrolls mounted on thin cylinders of wood; unrolled with the right hand as they were read, and rolled up with the left; seldom over 100 pages long], 43, *43*

Bridges, 23, *30*, 31, *31*

Britain, 24, 25

Camps, *26*, 27, *27*, *32*, 33, *33*, 34, *34*, 45

Cauponae (kau′pắn.ĭ) [inns, generally located near the gates of cities. They were laid out so that wagons could drive directly into wagon rooms; stables, toilets, wine rooms and proprietor's rooms were on the same floor; bedrooms were frequently on the second floor], 20, *20*, 21, *21*

Causeway, 40, *40*

Centurion [an officer in the legion], 22, *22*, 24, *24*, 27, *27*, 28, *28*, 35

Chairs
 basket, *2*
 benches, 8, *8*, *13*, *52*, *53*
 cathedra [armless with curved back], *2*
 currule [folding stool with curved legs and cushion], *17*, 35

Cloaks [various lengths, widths, and colors, with and without attached hoods; worn by men and women, citizens and non-citizens, soldiers and civilians], *2*, *3*, *6*, *7*, *8*, *9*, *11*, *16*, *17*, *18*, 23, *32*, 35, *46*, *47*, *50*, *51*

Cohort [one of the ten divisions of a legion], 17

Coins, 1; *see also* Sesterce

Colonia Agrippina (kắ.lô′né.ắ ắg.rĭ.pé′nắ) [a frontier fortress which became the modern city of Cologne, Germany], 22, *22*, 23

Columbaria (kŏl′ŭm.bā′rĭ.ắ), *18*, 19

Combs [used as hair ornaments by women. They were made of silver, gold, boxwood, ivory, or tortoise shell], 21, *21*

Communication, 1, 6, 19, 25, 35
 Acta Diurna [government news], 13

Compluvium (kŏm.plōō′vĭ.ŭm) [rectangular opening in roof of *domus* to admit rainwater], *2*

Consul [presiding officer of the senate (2)], 52, *52*

Cornwall [southwestern England], 29

Couch *(lectus)*
 as bed, *3*
 for dining, *3*

Courier, 35, *35*

Cuirass [body armor made of bands of iron joined by leather straps worn by soldiers in battle and drill], *23*, *28*

Curia [Senate building], 52, *52; see also* Roman Forum

Customs House, *37*

Dinner [A typical dinner party had nine people reclining on three couches around one table. The meal started about 4 P.M. and lasted for several hours. There were three main parts to the meal — at a simple meal for close friends there was probably one course for each part; more elaborate dinners could run into many courses for each part. In either case, the dinner started with *gustus* (appetizers), such as onions, lettuce, tuna, eggs, anchovies served with *mulsum* (wine sweetened with honey), followed by *cena*, the meal proper, at which might be served kid, chicken, cold ham, green beans, young cabbage sprouts, and wine with water. This would be followed by the *secunda mensa* (dessert), usually fresh fruit and nuts served with wine], 3, *3*

Egypt, 37, 40

Egyptians, 38, *38*, 39, 42

Emperor, 1, 5, 9, 19, 35, 41, 42, 45, 46, 49, 51

Excubitorium (ex.kōō.bĭ.tô′rē.ŭm), 17, *17*

Firemen, *see Vigili*

Flavian Amphitheatre *(Colosseum)* [Built in 80 A.D. it was 157 feet high, oval in shape; its exterior was faced with marble, and had niches containing painted statues], 9, *9*, *10*, 11, *11*

Floors
 hollow tiles in public baths, *13*
 mosaic in private house, *2*, *3*, *51*
 paved in apartment house, *38*

Fortifications, 22, 23, 25, *26*, 27, *27*, 28, *32*, 33, *33*, *44*, 45, *45*

Forum [public meeting place of great importance], 4, 5, *5*, 6, 27, 52

 Forum of Trajan [consisted of an equestrian statue of Trajan, the Basilica Ulpia (great courthouse), the Column of Trajan, two public libraries, one Latin, the other Greek, and the Temple of Trajan], 6, *6*, 7

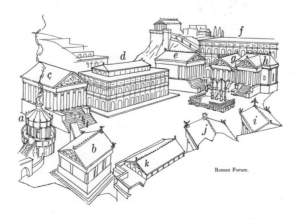

Roman Forum.